50 Quick and Easy Ways to Outstanding

Group Work

By Mike Gershon

About the Author

Mike Gershon is a teacher, trainer and writer. He is the author of twenty books on teaching, learning and education, including a number of bestsellers, as well as the co-author of one other. Mike's online resources have been viewed and downloaded more than 2.5 million times by teachers in over 180 countries and territories. He is a regular contributor to the Times Educational Supplement and has created a series of electronic CPD guides for TES PRO. Find out more, get in touch and download free resources at www.mikegershon.com

Training and Consultancy

Mike is an expert trainer whose sessions have received acclaim from teachers across England. Recent bookings include:

- *Improving Literacy Levels in Every Classroom*, St Leonard's Academy, Sussex

- *Growth Mindsets, Effective Marking and Feedback* Ash Manor School, Aldershot

- *Effective Differentiation,* Tri-Borough Alternative Provision (TBAP), London

Mike also works as a consultant, advising on teaching and learning and creating bespoke materials for schools. Recent work includes:

- *Developing and Facilitating Independent Learning,* Chipping Norton School, Oxfordshire

- *Differentiation In-Service Training,* Charles Darwin School, Kent

If you would like speak to Mike about the services he can offer your school, please get in touch by email: mike@mikegershon.com

Other Works from the Same Authors

Available to buy now on Amazon:

How to use Differentiation in the Classroom: The Complete Guide

How to use Assessment for Learning in the Classroom: The Complete Guide

How to use Questioning in the Classroom: The Complete Guide

How to use Discussion in the Classroom: The Complete Guide

How to Teach EAL Students in the Classroom: The Complete Guide

More Secondary Starters and Plenaries

Secondary Starters and Plenaries: History

Teach Now! History: Becoming a Great History Teacher

The Growth Mindset Pocketbook (with Professor Barry Hymer)

How to be Outstanding in the Classroom

Also available to buy now on Amazon, the entire 'Quick 50' Series:

50 Quick and Brilliant Teaching Ideas

50 Quick and Brilliant Teaching Techniques

50 Quick and Easy Lesson Activities

50 Quick Ways to Help Your Students Secure A and B Grades at GCSE

50 Quick Ways to Help Your Students Think, Learn, and Use Their Brains Brilliantly

50 Quick Ways to Motivate and Engage Your Students

50 Quick Ways to Outstanding Teaching

50 Quick Ways to Perfect Behaviour Management

50 Quick and Brilliant Teaching Games

50 Quick and Easy Ways to Outstanding Group Work

50 Quick and Easy Ways to Prepare for Ofsted

50 Quick and Easy Ways Leaders can Prepare for Ofsted

About the Series

The 'Quick 50' series was born out of a desire to provide teachers with practical, tried and tested ideas, activities, strategies and techniques which would help them to teach brilliant lessons, raise achievement and engage and inspire their students.

Every title in the series distils great teaching wisdom into fifty bite-sized chunks. These are easy to digest and easy to apply – perfect for the busy teacher who wants to develop their practice and support their students.

Acknowledgements

As ever I must thank all the fantastic colleagues and students I have worked with over the years, first while training at the Institute of Education, Central Foundation Girls' School and Nower Hill High School and subsequently while working at Pimlico Academy and King Edward VI School in Bury St Edmunds.

Thanks also to Alison and Andrew Metcalfe for a great place to write and finally to Gordon at KallKwik for help with the covers.

Table of Contents

Envoys

Marketplace

Presentations

Jigsaw Groups

Structured Discussion

Using Mini-Activities

Controlling Timings

Communicating with Groups

Circulating

State the Outcomes

Not Everyone Can Work Together

Have Extension Work Ready

Train Students how to do Group Work

Take a Step Back

Make Sure All Group Members Have a Clear Role

Be Ready to Intervene

Sometimes You Will Have to Decide

Clear Success Criteria

Know What Progress Looks Like (And Communicate This)

Peer-Assessment

Changing Groups

Removing Students

Focus on the Small Things

Introduction

Welcome to '50 Quick and Easy Ways to Outstanding Group Work.'

This book is all about that most wonderful of classroom activities: group work. It is through group work that some of the best learning takes place. Often, outstanding group work achieves outcomes that simply aren't possible through any other means.

In order to make sure group work is outstanding, you need guidance, advice and practical strategies. That is what this book offers.

All the entries provide something tangible you can use to develop and improve the group work which goes on in your classroom. Every entry is clear and concise, easy to implement and based on my extensive experience as a teacher and trainer.

Outstanding group work may not happen overnight. But it will happen if you work at it. Especially if you put into practice the activities, strategies and techniques outlined in this book.

So read on and enjoy! I hope you and your students achieve the very best outcomes as a result of your fantastic use of group work.

Begin with Great Planning

01 Outstanding group work is underpinned by great planning. In order to facilitate successful interactions between students, you need to first think about how those interactions will be structured and managed.

The purpose of planning is to assist our future selves. By doing things beforehand we can increase the likelihood that, when the time comes, we will be set up for success. Of course, the best plan in the world can unravel. However, operating with a plan is nearly always preferable to the opposite.

This is especially true of group work, where a number of issues can arise that may not play such a prominent role in other activity types.

Over the next few entries we will consider various important aspects of planning before going on to look at different elements of group work. The emphasis will be practical throughout.

Why are you using group work?

02 This is the first question to ask. Once you know the answer, you are in a much stronger position. This is because you have defined a clear and specific purpose for the group work. You can use this as a lens through which to plan, assess and teach.

Examples of why we use group work include:

- To facilitate positive student-student interactions.

- To promote active learning through pupil engagement.

- To provide students with the opportunity to work together.

- To give variation to our lessons.

- To achieve more learning and progress than would be possible through other means.

Other reasons also exist. Furthermore, you may have multiple reasons for using group work, rather than just one.

Whatever is the case, by stating clearly why you are using group work you will be placing yourself in a strong position from which to plan, teach and assess effectively.

Plan for Progress

03 Progress is at the heart of everything we do as teachers. If students make progress, they learn. It's as simple as that. If they don't make progress, something has gone wrong – and we need to deal with that.

When planning group work it is a good idea to plan for progress. This will help you to ensure the group work is successful, relevant and tied to the wider objective of making great learning happen.

You can plan for progress in various ways. These include:

- Working out what the objective is for the group work.

- Deciding how you will assess whether the objective has been achieved or not.

- Considering how you will assess the progress of individuals and groups during the course of the group work.

- Identifying clear success criteria for the task.

- Stating what it is you want pupils to get from the group work (which may include reference to both content and skills).

Plan for Problems

04 Initially, this sounds counter-intuitive. After all, planning is designed to eliminate problems, isn't it?

Well, yes, up to a point. Truthfully though, planning is as much about working out how to deal with and overcome problems as it is avoiding them. This is because there will always be things which are outside our control.

For example: the attitudes students bring to the lesson, the way in which pupils respond to the work and the speed at which students get to grips with the material.

Therefore, to secure outstanding group work it is vital we try to foresee potential problems and plan in advance how we will deal with them.

This approach is effective in all areas of life, not least when dealing with group work.

Plan for Yourself

05 Our final planning point concerns planning for yourself.

By this I mean that we should plan group work which takes account of what we want to achieve. So, for example, we need to think about issues such as:

- How we will move between groups.

- Whether we will be able to work with every group or not.

- If it will be possible to ensure maximum progress for everybody.

- How we can set up the group work so as to maximise the efficacy of our own time.

- What we will do if problems arise (see the last entry).

Your own role within group work can be easily overlooked. As such, it is necessary to flag it up as an important area of consideration during the planning process.

Using Resources

06 We now segue from general planning to some of the more practical aspects of group work, the first of which is resources.

Nearly all group work involves the use of resources.

It goes without saying that outstanding group work requires the teacher to have well-organised, high-quality resources. Not only should these be appropriate to the task and well-made, but they should also be matched to the needs of your group.

And, of course, you should have them printed out, arranged and ready to go before the lesson begins!

One word of warning. I have seen many excellent group work activities fall down under the weight of too many resources. It is advisable to ask on each occasion whether you could make life simpler for students by using fewer resources. If the answer is yes, then do this.

Checklist of Tasks

07 Here is a great way to help students succeed in group work and, in the process, secure significant progress.

Having decided on the nature of your group work task (and for various example tasks see later in this book as well as 50 Quick and Easy Lesson Activities), create a checklist containing the various sub-tasks that each group will need to complete in order to be successful.

You can then use this checklist during the group work activity. Either display it on the board or print out copies to hand to the different groups in your class.

Pupils can work through the checklist, safe in the knowledge that by doing so they will be successfully completing the wider task.

Teach Processes

08 Group work involves various processes we tend not to encounter in other activity types. These include:

- Getting into groups

- Working with a number of other students

- Dividing work up between different people

- Managing time as part of a team

- Taking on different roles

We might assume that pupils will know how to do all of this automatically. But why would they?

A better approach is to explicitly teach the various processes so that pupils know precisely what is expected of them, how to go about meeting these expectations and what needs to be done in order to make group work most effective.

Teaching the processes will take a little time at first. However, after the initial input you will reap significant rewards.

Group Sizes

09 We come now to the most basic aspect of group work: group sizes.

It is generally held that groups of three or four students are preferable. This is for a number of reasons.

First, the larger a group gets, the easier it is for some pupils to engage in social loafing, whereby they sit back and allow their peers to do all the work. Second, larger numbers make it harder for everybody to feel involved. Third, bigger groups are more difficult for the teacher to manage.

So, overall, it is best to stick to groups which are three or four students in number.

Using Time Limits

10 Time limits are a handy tool on which to call if you think your pupils will struggle to keep on track during group work.

Some students find it difficult to come to decisions. Others may take far too long on one sub-task and then neglect another.

Setting time limits means pupils know exactly what they need to do and when this needs to be done by.

You can set time limits for individual sub-tasks, for the group work activity as a whole or for specific groups. In the latter case, this serves to support students who struggle with time management without altering the working practices of the rest of the class.

Selecting Groups – Using Data

11 Over the next few entries we will consider various ways in which to select groups. To begin, let us look at using data.

By data we mean the information you have about students concerning their prior attainment, attendance, behavioural issues, SEN, FSM, EAL and G and T status. In most schools, all of this is accessible electronically through a database system such as Sims.

You can use this data to help you select groups. It is often most useful at the beginning of the year when you do not yet know your class. However, it is also a useful touchstone through the course of your teaching. For example, you might go back to the data after the Christmas holidays in order to refine or alter the groups you tend to use.

Selecting Groups Randomly: 3 Methods

12 Sometimes you may wish to select groups at random. Here are three simple methods you can use:

- Decide how many groups you want and then count students off using the same number. For example, if you want five groups of three in a class of fifteen, count 1 to 5 for the first five students, then for the second five and then for the third five. All the 1's then get together, all the 2's and so on.

- Ask students to line up according to some criteria (such as age or shoe size). Walk along the line counting out groups.

- Decide how many groups you want and of what size. For example, five groups of three. Cut up different coloured pieces of card into squares. You need the same number of pieces for each group (3 red, 3 green, 3 blue, 3 yellow and 3 orange in this case). Place the pieces in a bag and get pupils to pick one out at random. Pupils with the same colour form into groups.

Refining Groups

13 It may be that, having decided on your groups, you realise that you need to refine them. This may become apparent immediately or it may begin to surface after some time goes past.

In any case, the message is the same. Do not let things fester. Be ready to refine your groups quickly and confidently. This will send a clear message to your class that group work is focussed on learning and that the groups themselves must always be subordinated to this aim.

Using Specific Goals to Select Groups

14 Another way in which to select groups involves using a specific goal. Examples include:

- Wanting certain students to work together.

- Wanting to cultivate a particular atmosphere.

- Wanting to give certain students greater support.

- Wanting to improve behaviour.

- Wanting to avoid certain friendship groups (which lead to the pupils involved going off task).

If you can identify a specific goal which you want to achieve, use this as a means by which to plan your groups. However, do bear in mind that over time the groups you have chosen may no longer continue to meet that goal. Therefore, you may need to refine the groups at a later stage so as to ensure the goal is continually met.

Mixed Ability vs. Ability Grouping

15 Ability grouping means students are grouped according to their attainment levels. Mixed ability grouping does not take this into account.

Often, whether or not to use ability grouping comes down to a teacher's own values. You will need to decide whether you are happy grouping pupils according to ability or whether you feel that mixed ability grouping is more appropriate.

Personally, I take a pragmatic approach. Generally I use mixed groups however on certain occasions or with certain content I change to ability-based groups. Ultimately there is no cut and dried approach here. You will need to make a judgement call based on your pupils and the work you want them to do.

Secret Missions

16 We now move on to think about practical strategies you can use to make group work engaging and effective.

Secret missions create a great sense of excitement. Through this excitement they motivate students. An atmosphere of spectacle is generated; something different from the everyday; a little spice amid the fare to which we are accustomed.

Print off the instructions for your group work task and place these in a brown envelope. Write the words 'Secret Mission' on the front. Hand these out to your groups, making a big play of the secret nature of their missions. Some good results should ensue.

Develop the activity by giving different groups different secret missions to complete.

Competition

17 Introducing a competitive element to group work tasks can often have a positive effect. This is not always the case so you are advised to monitor the response of your classes. Some will respond well, others might be put off by the advent of a competitive environment.

Competition can be introduced in many forms. Examples include:

- Setting a time limit for the group work task and making it a race to see who can finish first.

- Setting a goal for the task which groups try to reach first.

- Setting a series of success criteria which need to be fulfilled by every group. You can then judge which group has fulfilled them most successfully.

Activities which Break Down

18 In entry seven we looked at the benefits of creating task checklists pupils can use to navigate their way through a group work task. In general, activities which can be easily broken down into smaller parts are a good basis for group work.

Two options are open to you.

First, you can break large activities down into a series of mini-tasks which groups work through in order. Second, you can break activities down into a series of separate tasks which are then assigned to different members of each group.

In both cases, the breaking up of the task makes it easier for pupils to engage with the work. In the second case, dividing the work between different group members means that everyone has a clear goal for which they are responsible.

Start with the Product

19 A different way to think about group work involves working backwards. Instead of planning forwards, plan from the finish.

Start by asking yourself what product you want groups to create. Then, work backwards step-by-step. This process will allow you to develop a task which results in all groups achieving a successful and effective product (which, in turn, will show that they have learned and made progress).

For example, you may decide you want groups to produce a presentation on one of Henry VIII's wives. Working back from this will allow you to compile a list of sub-tasks each group will need to complete in order to do so.

Task Mixture

20 Another way to encourage engagement in group work activities involves providing a mixture of tasks. These separate items go together to create the overall task. Here is an example:

Group Work Activity:

Design a leaflet explaining the benefits of wind farms

Sub-Tasks:

Research the benefits of wind farms

Create an attractive design for the leaflet

Design an interactive element such as a game or a quiz

Write the different sections of the leaflet

Illustrate the leaflet using images and diagrams

You will note here that we have a mixture of tasks – research, design, writing and illustration. This means students have the chance to engage with the work from different angles. They can also play to their own strengths where appropriate.

Essentially this is good differentiation – setting up a task so that it maximises the potential for success across the board (which in turn leads to significant learning gains).

Envoys

21 We will now look at five classic group work activities. You can find descriptions of these in some of my other books, but I repeat them here due to their relevance.

Envoys works as follows:

Divide the class into groups. Assign a topic to each group. Explain that groups must research their topics so they become experts. Give a time limit for this and provide the necessary resources.

When the time is up, invite each group to nominate an envoy. Envoys stand up and leave their groups. They move clockwise around the room, teaching all the other groups in the class one-by-one. This means that, eventually, everybody in the class has learned about every topic.

It is useful to supplement the activity with a pro-forma on which pupils can capture what they learn.

Marketplace

22 Divide the class into groups. Assign a research topic to each group. You might frame this as a research question they need to answer. Provide resources and a time limit in which groups have to complete their work.

When the time is up, indicate the class is to be transformed into a marketplace where learning can be traded. Each group will set up their own stall from where they can sell their learning to their peers.

When the marketplace has been created, invite groups to decide who will stay at the stall and who will leave. Those who leave go and visit the other stalls where they can trade their knowledge. This eventually results in everybody in the class learning about each of the topics.

Presentations

23 Presentations are a commonly used group work task in which pupils work together to create a presentation on a given topic.

You can make them more effective through the following:

- Provision of success criteria clearly identifying what the presentation should include.

- Insisting that presentations are fully rehearsed and refined prior to final delivery (set aside specific time in which students can do this).

- Requesting that a summary of key points is provided.

- Modelling good and bad presentation techniques for your pupils.

- Providing a breakdown of what sub-tasks need to be completed in order to produce a high-quality presentation.

Jigsaw Groups

24 Divide the class into groups of four. Ask groups to number themselves 1 – 4. Display four numbered questions or tasks on the board, all of which should connect to the topic of study. In each group, pupils are responsible for the numbered task/question which matches their number.

At this point, the original groups dissolve and new groups form.

The new groups are based on the numbers students have chosen. So, for example, all the number ones form a group, as do all the number twos and so on. The new groups then have a certain length of time to complete their task or answer their question (it may be necessary to divide the new groups up if you have a lot of students).

When sufficient time has passed, pupils return to their original groups. They now take it in turns to share what they have learned. This results in everybody learning about all the different questions or tasks.

Structured Discussion

25 Discussion is an excellent basis for group work. To make discussion effective, it generally needs to be structured. If not, there is the risk that it will descend into social chat, veer off course or lack the depth required for good progress to be made.

Here are five ways you can structure group discussion:

- Provide a series of questions which need to be discussed in turn.

- Provide a pro-forma one member of the group uses to make notes of the discussion.

- Appoint group leaders. It is their job to keep the discussion on topic.

- Provide question prompts which group members can use to move the discussion forwards.

- Break the discussion down into separate sections and set clear time limits for each part.

Using Mini-Activities

26 Pace and motivation are important in any lesson. They play a significant part in all outstanding teaching, including that centred on group work.

A nice way to maintain pace and motivation during group work tasks is to use a series of mini-activities, each lasting perhaps 5-7 minutes. These are introduced sequentially (rather than all at the beginning). With each new activity, pupils have to quickly think about what is being asked of them and then get down to the task in hand straight away.

Three or four connected mini-activities are often far more motivational for a lethargic class than one larger activity.

Ensure each mini-activity is more challenging than the last to be certain of sustained progress throughout the task.

Controlling Timings

27 Timings are crucial to outstanding group work. Through controlling these, you will find yourself well-placed to manage any activity such that it runs as effectively as possible.

A common mistake involves setting up timings and then sticking to these religiously. This is problematic because it fails to take account of changing circumstances and the evidence provided by your students. For example, if pupils are clearly struggling to complete a task you have set, it will be necessary for you to give them some more time.

Similarly, if it turns out that you overestimated the time required for a particular group task, you need to be ready to move things on quickly.

During group work activities, you should constantly monitor where your students are at and use the information you elicit to make judgements about timings.

Communicating with Groups

28 Communicating with the various groups in your class means you are able to keep them on track. Consider what happens if you don't communicate with your groups – you'll have no idea where they are up to!

Therefore, communicating regularly is a vital part of your role during group work. Communication should cover the following as a minimum:

- Finding out where groups are up to.

- Telling groups where they should be up to or what they need to do next.

- Using questioning to push the thinking of different groups.

- Helping groups to deal with problems and difficulties.

- Explaining and re-explaining both relevant content and the exact demands of the task.

Circulating

29 Circulating means moving around the room while students are working. This allows you to monitor, observe, question, support and elicit information. In the last case, you can use this information to adapt your teaching.

For example, you might note that a particular group are struggling with the work. You would then be in a position to give them close support and attention.

Circulating during group work is a great way to ensure that all pupils remain on task. It is also an excellent opportunity to listen in to the discussions pupils are having. These are often very revealing, allowing you to see clearly how students are thinking about a topic (including any misconceptions under which they may be labouring).

State the Outcomes

30 Group work often falls below outstanding because of a lack of clarity. Students who are not entirely sure as to what they are supposed to be doing are more likely to go off task, engage in social conversation or make less progress.

It is well worth sharing the outcomes you expect from the group work before the activity begins. The benefits are threefold.

First, this will give students a clear sense of purpose. They will know exactly what they are doing and precisely why they are doing it.

Second, it will give you a reference point to which you can refer during the course of the activity. So, for example, if one group go off topic, you can refer them back to the expected outcomes you stated at the start of the task.

Third, pupils will be able to measure their own progress against the outcomes as they work through the task. This will help them to regulate their own learning.

Not Everyone Can Work Together

31 This is well worth remembering. Some combinations of students just do not work. Sometimes the reason is obvious, sometimes it feels almost impossible to discern.

The best approach is to begin from the premise that not everyone can work together. Otherwise, you are likely to become frustrated or annoyed when combinations of pupils fail to produce the level of work you would like.

Bearing the premise in mind will help you to deal with dysfunctional groups. It will also keep you alive to the fact that you may need to change the make-up of your groups. Sometimes this even needs to be done on the hoof. If a situation is not working, you simply have to rectify it as soon as possible.

Have Extension Work Ready

32 As with individual or paired work, so with group work.

Inevitably, some groups will finish tasks before other groups. This might be because they are more able, because they have worked quicker or because, for some reason, they have grasped the work more easily.

Whatever causes one group to finish before another, by having extension work ready you will be in a position to stretch and challenge that particular group. Extension work can take the form of a further task, a question or a reflection activity in which pupils examine what they have done and how they might have done it better.

Train Students how to do Group Work

33 We talked in entry eight about the benefits of teaching students the processes inherent to group work. Here we revisit this idea in a slightly different context.

Training students how to do group work is all about maximising the chance that students will engage positively and effectively in any task you set. By training pupils, you will be embedding habits and ways of acting which help to achieve this goal.

For example, you might spend a whole lesson getting students to repeat different aspects of group work (moving into groups; assigning tasks; managing time and so on). This will then make it much easier for pupils to complete these aspects successfully in subsequent lessons.

I have even seen teachers design a specific approach to group work which is 'their way of doing things.' They then train all their students in this method so that they can apply it again and again over the course of a year.

Take a Step Back

34 One of the risks with group work is that you get drawn in to such an extent that you lose sight of the bigger picture. This is natural. You want pupils to succeed so you end up working closely with a group who need your help.

However, your ultimate aim is to ensure the greatest possible progress for the greatest number of students. Therefore, you need to retain a keen eye on the class as a whole. Otherwise, how do you know that everyone is learning?

So, remind yourself during group work activities to take a step back. This will allow you to see the big picture which, in turn, will help you to ensure that everybody is on track and learning throughout the course of the activity.

Make Sure All Group Members Have a Clear Role

35 If group members do not have a clear role, they may find themselves lost, uncertain and without a sense of purpose. This will result in them disengaging from the task. If this happens, the educational benefits of group work will disappear for those students.

There are a number of ways to ensure all group members have a clear role:

- Keep groups to 3 or 4 students. This avoids the situation where there is not enough work to keep all pupils occupied.

- Assign specific roles such as leader, timekeeper, scribe, motivator, devil's advocate and so forth. The roles you assign will need to be appropriate for the particular task you have set.

- Visit each group at the start of the activity and ask them to tell you who is doing what.

Be Ready to Intervene

36 If you identify a group who are not working positively, who have gone off task or who are, for whatever reason, disengaging from the task, you must be ready to intervene.

Rehearse in advance what you will say. For example: 'We need to get back on task because the purpose of what we're doing is learning.' Rehearsing this in advance makes it much easier to apply when the situation arises.

It is also worth enquiring why a group is not working as you would wish. This is not about them justifying their behaviour though. Rather, it is about identifying what has caused the behaviour and then assessing whether you can do anything to remove the problem.

Sometimes You Will Have to Decide

37 If a group is taking an age to decide how they will tackle a task or who is to do what, you may need to step in.

Sometimes we find that students cannot come to a decision. This is not unique to youngsters. The same behaviour can be observed in some adult groups. The reasons are usually tangled, encompassing social norms, perceived etiquette and inertia.

Should you come across a group who are not making progress with the task, step in and move them on by taking a decision on their behalf.

It is a good idea to preface this with something along the lines of: 'OK, you have two minutes to decide. If you haven't decided by then, I'll choose for you.' This way, you are giving pupils a chance before taking control yourself.

Clear Success Criteria

38 We have mentioned success criteria on a number of occasions so far. They are well worth their own entry due to the huge effect they can have on whether or not group work is successful.

Success criteria define what is good (and, at the same time, what is not good). As such, they convey to students a clear sense of what needs to be done if success is to be achieved. They minimise ambiguity, remove vagueness and provide clarity.

All of this is greatly beneficial. Success criteria help students appreciate precisely what is required of them. They also act as a point of reference pupils can use to self-regulate during the course of an activity.

Know What Progress Looks Like (And Communicate This)

39 If you know what progress looks like then you know what you are looking for.

If you know what progress looks like then you can tell students what they need to do to be successful (because you will define them as successful if they meet your expectations).

In group work, progress usually comprises developments in skills and content knowledge. The relative weighting of these varies from task to task.

Before beginning any group work activity, ask yourself what will constitute progress. Refine this idea, make it clear, and then convey it to your students. Repeatedly doing this should result in significant learning gains.

Peer-Assessment

40 Peer-assessment is worth using in all teaching. It opens up success criteria, exposes students to different work and helps them to develop a critical mindset.

In terms of group work, one of the best uses of peer-assessment involves pupils assessing the products that different groups produce. They do this by using a set of success criteria provided by the teacher.

A nice example of how this works is as follows. The teacher hands a collection of post-it notes to each group. Students leave their work on their desks and move off to see what other groups have created. They use their post-it notes to leave peer-assessment comments and, when they return to their own work, receive a series of comments in kind.

Changing Groups

41 It can be tempting to stick with groups that work. If it ain't broke, don't fix it. This logic is fine, up to a point.

Effective groups can work well over time. Students become familiar with their peers and learn how to work successfully with them.

At the same time, keeping groups as they are can result in a sense of staleness developing. Pupils fall into ruts – familiar ways of working in which the brain is no longer actively engaged.

It is therefore worthwhile changing groups on a fairly regular basis. This can involve something as simple as changing the groups for a couple of weeks before reverting back to how things were. Or, it might mean a regular cycle of changes (the corollary of which is that students will come to see group work as a time when they could be working with anybody).

Removing Students

42 During group work the teacher relinquishes some of the control they exert over the class. This is a good thing because, without doing this, group work is not particularly effective.

When we relinquish control, there is an increased likelihood that unwelcome or off-task behaviour will result. It is by no means certain, but the possibility is increased.

As with any teaching, so with group work. If a student does not meet your expectations, you must deal with this immediately. Do so calmly and assertively. Focus on the behaviour and give the student a choice. Make it clear that a negative choice on their part will lead to them being removed from the group work.

If such a choice is made, follow through. Take the student out of the group work task and set them some independent work to do.

The wider message is clear: group work requires positive behaviour focussed on the learning. If this is not forthcoming, consequences will result.

Focus on the Small Things

43 By focussing on the small things we avoid letting the big things happen.

For example, you might like to pick up any student who doesn't listen to what their fellow group member says (maybe they talk over them or ignore their input). By drawing attention to this and expecting the pupil to change their behaviour, you will be nipping things in the bud before they have the chance to get any more serious.

The same applies to all aspects of group work. Taking care of the small things means the big things rarely occur.

Monitoring Progress

44 If you find it tricky to monitor progress during group work activities, here are five simple methods you might like to try:

- Ask groups to provide you with status updates at specified points.

- Walk from group to group every 5-10 minutes. Ask each one to tell you where they are up to.

- Appoint group leaders. Ask these students to keep you informed of their group's progress.

- Make regular checks using thumbs. State where groups should be at. If a group is there or beyond, they give a thumbs up. If they are not there yet, they give a thumbs down.

- Hand out a task checklist. Ask groups to tick the tasks off as they go and to keep the checklist visible. When you circulate, make a note of what has been ticked off by each group.

Avoiding Ambiguity

45 Ambiguity decreases the quality of group work. If your instructions aren't clear, pupils will struggle to do what you want them to do. Similarly, if you do not communicate your expectations clearly, how can you expect students to meet them?

Pay attention to the language you use when speaking as well as that which is on your resources. If things aren't clear, change them.

Making Peace

46 Sometimes pupils argue. This is a fact of life. Group work can lead to conflicts, particularly if pupils are not used to dealing positively with disagreements.

In such instances, it is your job to make the peace. Intervene as early as possible to prevent things escalating. Remain calm, positive and assertive. State clearly what needs to occur and what the consequences will be if this does not happen.

Give pupils a chance to make the right choice. If they do not, intervene again and follow through on your consequences. Where appropriate, talk to the students involved after the lesson and help them to understand why what they did was wrong and how they can avoid acting in that way in the future.

Rehearsing Conflict Resolution and Problem Solving

47 We noted in the last entry that some pupils do not have the skills necessary to deal positively with disagreements.

There is a simple remedy for this: teach them!

Take some time to rehearse conflict resolution and problem solving techniques with your classes. Develop some dramatic scenarios pupils can use as practice. Show students what positive conflict resolution looks like. And then, if disagreements do develop during a group work task, remind pupils to use the methods they have learned to deal with these in a positive and mature way.

Provide a Conflict Resolution Structure

48 You can take things a step further by providing a conflict resolution structure. This is a model you ask all pupils to use whenever there is an issue during a group work task. Teach students the structure and then place a poster on your wall reminding them of how it works.

Here is an example:

Step 1: Take it in turns to speak.

Step 2: Listen actively when it is not your turn to speak.

Step 3: Remind yourselves what the goal of the activity is.

Step 4: Identify how each person's idea can contribute to that goal.

Step 5: Develop a compromise on which people can agree.

Teach Positive Language

49 If disagreements arise during group work, these are often exacerbated by the use of negative language. This sees students becoming emotional and connecting the disagreement to their own ego – sending them into defensive mode.

As part of your conflict resolution and problem solving training, teach students the importance of positive language. Give them exemplars they can use if they find themselves in a disagreement. Use drama to let students experience the difference between being spoken to positively and negatively.

You might also like to make posters for your walls modelling positive language. You can then refer pupils to these should they slip up during a group work activity.

Model Positive Interactions

50 We conclude our journey through 50 quick and easy ways to outstanding group work by returning to the one person who makes it all happen: you.

If you can model positive interactions throughout your time in the classroom, not just while group work is going on, you will be setting an excellent example for your students. This example will act as a model they can copy and to which you can refer them if their standards slip. It will also convey to all pupils the high expectations you have and just what it is that you want them to do in order to be successful.

And don't be afraid to draw attention to what you are doing. Sometimes students need things spelt out for them. So tell them that you are interacting positively and hammer home the benefits of this for everybody involved.

So now all that is left for me to say is that I hope you have found the activities, strategies and techniques in this book useful. And good luck in making your group work outstanding!

A Brief Request

If you have found this book useful I would be delighted if you could leave a review on Amazon to let others know.

If you have any thoughts or comments, or if you have an idea for a new book in the series you would like me to write, please don't hesitate to get in touch at mike@mikegershon.com.

Finally, don't forget that you can download all my teaching and learning resources for **FREE** at www.mikegershon.com.

Printed in Great Britain
by Amazon